EXPERIENCING
GOD'S PRESENCE

EXPERIENCING
GOD'S PRESENCE

Warren and Ruth Myers

NAVPRESS®

Bringing Truth to Life

OUR GUARANTEE TO YOU

We believe so strongly in the message of our books that we are making this quality guarantee to you. If for any reason you are disappointed with the content of this book, return the title page to us with your name and address and we will refund to you the list price of the book. To help us serve you better, please briefly describe why you were disappointed. Mail your refund request to: NavPress, P.O. Box 35002, Colorado Springs, CO 80935.

NavPress
P.O. Box 35001
Colorado Springs, Colorado 80935

The Navigators is an international Christian organization. Our mission is to reach, disciple, and equip people to know Christ and to make Him known through successive generations. We envision multitudes of diverse people in the United States and every other nation who have a passionate love for Christ, live a lifestyle of sharing Christ's love, and multiply spiritual laborers among those without Christ.

NavPress is the publishing ministry of The Navigators. NavPress publications help believers learn biblical truth and apply what they learn to their lives and ministries. Our mission is to stimulate spiritual formation among our readers.

ISBN 1-57683-418-2

Cover design by Ray Moore
Cover photo by Andrew Mounter
Creative Team: Paul Santhouse, Keith Wall, Darla Hightower, Pat Miller

Some of the anecdotal illustrations in this book are true to life and are included with the permission of the persons involved. All other illustrations are composites of real situations, and any resemblance to people living or dead is coincidental.

Unless otherwise identified, all Scripture quotations in this publication are taken from the *New American Standard Bible* (NASB), © The Lockman Foundation 1960, 1962, 1963, 1968, 1971, 1972, 1973, 1975, 1977; Other versions used include: the *Modern Language Bible: The Berkeley Version in Modern English* (MLB), copyright © Zondervan Publishing House 1945, 1959, 1969, used by permission; *The New Testament in Modern English* (PH), J. B. Phillips Translator, © J. B. Phillips 1958, 1960, 1972, used by permission of Macmillan Publishing Company; *The Living Bible* (TLB), Copyright © 1971, used by permission of Tyndale House Publishers, Inc., Wheaton, IL 60189, all rights reserved; and the *King James Version* (KJV).

Printed in Canada

1 2 3 4 5 6 7 8 9 10 / 07 06 05 04 03

FOR A FREE CATALOG OF
NAVPRESS BOOKS & BIBLE STUDIES,
CALL 1-800-366-7788 (USA)
OR 1-416-499-4615 (CANADA)

CONTENTS

AS YOU BEGIN

G OD IS INTENSELY INTERESTED in us as persons. The fact that He has given us a special book reveals His longing to communicate with us in a personal way and to draw us into His presence. An appropriate title for the Bible could be *God's Involvement with People,* and one persistent message from God radiates from its pages:

> My heart is involved with all of you. Even before I created man I planned the highest, most convincing demonstration of My love—the sending of My Son to die for people who would rebel against Me and have no use for Me. I sent Him to make possible an intimate relationship with Me for every person born. Always I search for individuals who will respond to Me and enter into My purposes. I draw such persons to Me with cords of love, and I commit Myself to a faithful, enduring relationship with each of them. As they consent to be involved with Me, I lift them to a life of enjoyment and significance—in this world and in eternity.

How astonishing that this majestic, sovereign God yearns to be involved with us and longs to meet our needs! Repeatedly He reveals Himself to be our Father and Friend, our Redeemer and Rescuer, our Provider and Guide and Protector. He is bread to satisfy our hunger, water to quench our thirst. He offers to meet not only our physical and social needs, but also the deepest needs of our total natures. Now and forever, He wants to make us feel secure, valued, and significant.

He asks us to relate to Him as children. When a child relates to another person, his attitude is one of dependence and his interests center on his own personal needs. If he could formulate his thoughts, he might ask, "What needs of mine will this person meet? What are his feelings and attitudes toward me? Can I depend on him?"

The question "What needs of mine will God meet?" is always appropriate, for He asks us to recognize our dependence on Him and say, "Give us this day what we need."

But if our relationship with Him is to mature to new levels of satisfaction, other questions must also arise: "What can I be to Him? What needs of His can I meet? What purposes of His can I share?" For some of us, such questions inspire fear. We ask, "Will this awesome, all-powerful God use me for His own ends? What would it cost me?" For others, the questions seem out of place or even absurd. They ask, "How can a self-existent, all-sufficient God need anything? What could I possibly give Him? All things come from Him, and anything I 'give' Him is already His. If He were in need or hungry, He would not ask me, for He owns 'the cattle on a thousand hills.'"

This is indeed absurd if you define *need* as "anything required for existence or well-being." In that sense God has no needs. But *need* also means "anything desired or useful." God has desires; He is love and He longs for our love. From eternity He has fastened His affection on us and set us apart for Himself, for intimate delights and exciting purposes. From eternity He has planned a family for Himself and a bride for His Son. As a devoted father needs his child's nearness, and as a loving bridegroom needs his bride's responsiveness, so God needs us.

This study book will help you find authentic and gratifying answers to the questions "What is God to me?" and "What can I be to Him?" It will point you to ways you can respond to God and experience His reality more fully. As you study, ask God to free you from misconceptions about Him. Ask Him to convert any correct-but-cold concepts you may have about Him into soul-gripping realities that will change your life. Pray that the Holy Spirit will guide you into new levels of personal involvement with the Lord and His truth.

Perhaps at present you cannot approach God with an attitude of full commitment. Maybe the very thought of deep involvement frightens you; you want genuine love but find it hard to trust anyone. Perhaps, deep inside, you are afraid that God will diminish you as a person or ask you to make sacrifices that are too great. If you have such fears or reservations, begin to seek God just as you are, being honest with Him about your feelings. Give Him opportunity, through His Word, to resolve your doubts, to melt your inner barriers with His love, and to involve Himself with you in daily and lifelong satisfaction.

Any satisfying relationship demands time and teamwork. It requires cultivation, often at the cost of eliminating urgent or important interests of lesser value. God has made all the first moves to establish a close relationship, and now it's up to you. Your day-by-day choices will govern the richness of your relationship with Him.

May your roots go down deep into the soil of God's marvelous love; and may you be able to feel and understand, as all God's children should, how long, how wide, how deep, and how high His love really is; and to experience this love for yourselves, though it is so great that you will never see the end of it or fully know or understand it. (Ephesians 3:17-19, TLB)

HOW TO DO THE
EXPERIENCING GOD STUDY

T HIS BIBLE STUDY AND meditation series has been designed to open for you new and exciting avenues of biblical understanding and to help you apply the truths you discover. Each of the topics is divided into two studies. The first, the *Experiencing God Study,* will begin to give you a rich grasp of one aspect of being involved with God; the optional *Additional Experiencing God Study* will enable you to understand the same aspect more deeply.

In order to discover and apply these truths about involvement with God, you will need to spend time meditating and praying over the Scripture passages. Approach the study expectantly, relying on the Holy Spirit to guide you in your desire to know God better. To further enrich your understanding, do each chapter yourself and then meet with a group that has also done it. Discuss your discoveries and applications with one another.

AIDS TO YOUR STUDY

As your main Bible, use a basic version such as the *King James Version,* the *New American Standard Bible,* the *New International Version,* or the *Revised Standard Version.* You can then enrich your study by referring to one or more of the other versions and paraphrases presently available, such as *The Message* by Eugene Peterson, *The New Testament in Modern English* by J. B. Phillips, the *Modern Language Bible: The Berkeley Version,* the *New English Bible,* and *The New Living Translation.*

Begin with the *Experiencing God Study,* and then go on to the *Additional Experiencing God Study* if you desire to pursue the topic further.

You may keep this book in its original binder, or photocopy the pages and insert them in a loose-leaf notebook in order to have room for additional pages to record long answers, prayer requests, illustrations, and personal observations.

(For additional materials that can help you in personal meditation and Bible study and in group discussion, see *For Further Reading,* page 105.)

PARTS OF YOUR STUDY

Each study is divided into five parts. Before you begin your first study, reread the *As You Begin* section of this book, marking the truths that stand out to you. Each time you do a study, you may find it profitable to review the highlights you have marked.

Following are helps in how to do each part of the study.

1. Verses to Consider

The Bible verses listed in this part are the ones you will use for the topic you are considering. Study them in the sequence listed as preparation for part 2.

Look up each verse or passage in two or three translations, if possible, and meditate carefully on each one. Meditation, a key ingredient of this study, involves taking time to allow God to speak to you. In your meditation, analyze what each verse is saying by emphasizing different words in the verse, putting the verse into your own words, or asking your own questions about it. As truths about God stand out to you, examine your life and see what bearing they may have on your attitudes and actions. As you meditate, mark in your Bible(s) the things that most impress you.

2. Favorite Passages

Reexamine the passages you have marked in your Bible and choose the verses or phrases that most help you understand and feel the reality of the truth you are studying. Copy these in this part of your study. In the future, add other Scriptures that speak to you in a definite way about seeking God. Use this part often for meditation and praise.

Aim to record a few truths that particularly impress you rather than copying all the passages. After you tune in your heart to this aspect of God's presence, you will be more alert to finding additional Scriptures as you have your quiet time, listen to messages, and discuss the Word with your friends. By adding new verses when you find them, you can expand your study in the coming days, months, and even years. Insert additional blank pages as you need them.

Take time to appreciate and worship God in connection with the truths you are discovering. Appreciation and worship are vitally important—they uplift your spirit and bring pleasure and glory to God. Cultivate the habit of turning often to the *Favorite Passages* part of your studies for further reflection and praise. You can do this at the beginning of your quiet time, in family devotions, or before going to bed. Return to these parts also when you need fresh motivation in experiencing God's presence.

For the topic *Maintaining Fellowship with His People,* your Favorite Passages part might look like this:

2. Favorite Passages: Copy from your Bible the verses or parts of verses that mean most to you from the *Verses to Consider* section. (In the future, add other Scriptures that speak to you in a definite way about seeking God. Use this part often for meditation and praise.)

"And let us think of [bestow thought on] one another and how we can encourage each other to love and do good deeds. And let us not hold aloof from our church meetings, as some do. Let us do all we can to help one another's faith, and this the more earnestly as we see the final day drawing nearer." (Hebrews 10:24-25, PH)

"With all humility and gentleness, with patience, showing forbearance to one another in love, [be] diligent to preserve the unity of the Spirit in the bond of peace." (Ephesians 4:2-3)

"Wherefore receive ye one another, as Christ also received us to the glory of God." (Romans 15:7, KJV)

3. Observations, Illustrations, and Quotations

After you copy your favorite passages, meditate on them, asking the Lord for fresh understanding. Think about them phrase by phrase, using a dictionary to clarify the meaning of words you do not fully understand. Record your main thoughts and meditations in this part. As you continue studying, you may also collect quotations, poems, and illustrations that will enrich your appreciation of the topic being studied. For illustrations, be especially alert to ways in which the Lord Jesus and other Bible personalities, outstanding Christians of the past and present, spiritual leaders, your Christian friends, and you yourself have practiced or taught this truth.

4. How This Truth Can Affect My Life (Application)

Pray that you will increasingly relate to God day-by-day in the way these Scriptures suggest. Ask yourself, *In what specific way can any of my favorite passages help me in one of the following areas?*

- In gaining an increased sense of my importance to God
- In overcoming fears, anxieties, discouragements, negative attitudes
- In facing trials and overcoming difficulties
- In cultivating positive emotions and loving attitudes
- In finding the fulfillment of my longings
- In representing God and helping others grow spiritually

For the topic *Maintaining Fellowship with His People,* your application might read like this:

4. How This Truth Can Affect My Life (Application)

The Lord has impressed me that often I don't make allowances for the things others do (Ephesians 4:2). Sometimes when other people hurt me or overlook my needs, I talk to God with a chip on my shoulder: "Well, You love me even if they don't." I forget that God dearly loves them too and longs for me to mend relationships rather than withdraw. Since Sunday I've had a grudge against several friends for not including me in an after-church get-together. I have now decided to make allowances for what seemed inconsiderate, to pray that the Lord will bless them in special ways, and to watch for some way to be helpful to at least one of them.

Applying the Scriptures to daily living is a major goal of Bible study. Applications in this study answer the question "What does this aspect of experiencing God's presence say to *me?*" Many consider this the most valuable part of the study, because it provides practical ways to be involved with God in your everyday life and can become a stepping-stone to greater fruitfulness.

An application may be drawn from one phrase, one verse, or the whole study. When you write, use the personal singular pronouns "I," "me," "my," and "mine." Your application should be practical and specific. It should concern a truth you can translate into your daily attitudes, worship, relationships, or activities. State it clearly enough to be understood if you were to read it to a friend or in a discussion group.

Here are a few examples of possible steps to take: Memorize the verse that especially speaks to you and review it daily with praise and prayer; say "yes" to God on some specific issue; say "no" to some activity or relationship that hinders your spiritual growth; go to a friend or loved one, confessing an offense and asking forgiveness; ask a friend or spiritual leader to pray for you in the specific need involved; begin your quiet time each day for a week with prayer about the matter that concerns you; decide to begin some new habit in experiencing God's presence, such as a regular quiet time, consistent Scripture memory, or a monthly half-day of prayer.

5. Future Study

During such activities as church services, Bible studies, or informal discussions, you may come across passages of Scripture that apply to the topics you have studied. You may not have time to copy them in the *Favorite Passages* parts, so jot down the references in this part for later study and use.

NOTE: If you decide to spend more time on this study, proceed to the *Additional Experiencing God Study* on this subject. The next section contains instructions for doing the additional study.

HOW TO DO THE *ADDITIONAL EXPERIENCING GOD STUDY*

THE OPTIONAL *ADDITIONAL EXPERIENCING God Study* has been designed to help you go deeper in your involvement with God. Its seven sections challenge you to study and meditate on the same topic in greater depth than in the initial study. Through this additional study you will learn further methods for studying the Bible and will grow to understand in a fuller way how each topic relates to your own life and the lives of others. This can be the richest part of your study.

The following instructions apply to all of the studies of this book except topics 1 and 8, *Seeking Him* and *Obeying Him,* for which specific questions have been designed.

1. LOOK UP THE FOLLOWING VERSES. Meditate on them and then add the most meaningful portions to your *Favorite Passages.* As an option, find additional verses on your own.

Refer again to the instructions for *Verses to Consider* and *Favorite Passages* on pages 12-13. To find additional verses, use cross-references from your own memory, the margins of your Bible, or a concordance. If you desire to meditate more intensively, use the six great observation questions: Who? What? When? Where? Why? How? The following sample questions give you ideas on how to do this. Use as few or as many as are helpful, and think of other questions also.

- WHO?
  Who in this passage responded to God?
- WHAT?
  What is God like in attributes, attitudes, desires?

What does He want to do for me?

What does He want me to do?

* WHEN?

When should I respond to God in this way?

* WHERE?

Where should I envision myself as God's child?

Where does God promise to be?

* WHY?

Why is it important for God and me to be more intimately involved with each other?

* HOW?

How does God feel about me?

How did some person in this passage relate to God?

How can I more effectively respond to God?

Jot down on another piece of paper the answers you especially want to remember.

2. Write a paragraph or simple outline summarizing what your *Favorite Passages* (and possibly other verses you have considered) say about this topic.

In your summary paragraph or outline, briefly state in your own words the important points from the passages. In this part, do not include any personal ideas or interpretation, but only what the Bible actually says. An example for the topic *Maintaining Fellowship with His People* might look like this in summary form:

> God wants His people to meet together, encouraging one another, sharing rich truths from His Word, using the gifts He has given for uplifting and serving. We are to demonstrate humility, patience, love, honesty, and concern about others' interests. We are to be diligent in preserving unity, to be alert in seeking forgiveness and making allowances for faults, and to receive others as Christ received us. United, edifying fellowship glorifies God and develops His people, who are His dwelling place on earth.

Sometimes you may enjoy making a summary outline, recording first the main divisions of the topic and then summarizing the content of the verses under these headings. For the previous topic, your summary outline might read:

> *I. Why We Must Meet with God's People*
>
> *God wants His people to meet together so that they can encourage one another, share rich truths from His Word, and use their gifts to uplift and serve one another. Loving, united fellowship glorifies God and develops His people, who are His dwelling place on earth.*
>
> *II. How We Must Relate to God's People*
>
> *We are to relate to one another with humility, patience, love, honesty, and concern for one another's interests. We are to be diligent in preserving unity, to be alert in seeking forgiveness and making allowances for faults, and to receive others as Christ received us.*

3. IN YOUR *FAVORITE PASSAGES* what truths stand out to you about God and His involvement with you, such as His relationship to you, His attributes, His attitudes, His desires, His promises, and His actions?

Some sample answers might be:

For chapter 2, *Depending on Him*:

> *I was impressed in Hebrews 4:16 that God is fully and immediately approachable even when I have failed Him, ready to be merciful to me and graciously help me. Other passages showed Him to be utterly reliable as my protector, my deliverer, and my supplier of strength and power.*

For chapter 3, *Communing with Him*:

> *How valuable His love is to me!*
>
> *How abundantly He wants to satisfy and delight me! (Psalm 36:7-8)*

For chapter 4, *Listening to His Word*:

> *The account of Mary and Martha in Luke 10 showed me how much the Lord values having me sit at His feet and listen to His words. Several other verses impressed me with how communicative God is — as He has*

shown by providing His Word and His Spirit so that I can know and understand His thoughts.

4. ANSWER ONE OR BOTH of the following:
   a. What thoughts, feelings, attitudes, or reservations have hindered me from [the topic being studied]?

   b. Although my conscious mind may agree that [the topic being studied] is important, do my daily choices and actions demonstrate my belief? What changes in my schedule or in my manner of relating to God does He want me to make?

For a., one answer on the topic of *Confiding in Him* might be:

> *I've often had the feeling that God was too great or too busy to be interested in my daily needs and feelings and the small details of my life.*

For b., a possible answer on the same topic may be:

> *Whenever I'm distressed or perplexed or lonely, I always pick up the phone or go see a friend instead of opening up to God. I feel He wants me to talk my problems over with Him first from now on.*

5. WRITE A BRIEF STATEMENT about some truth that impresses you in this study, for frequent use in experiencing God's presence.

This "statement of truth" can help you get a grip on a particular truth in a useable way so that it can rescue you when contrary thoughts, feelings, desires, or distractions hinder your response to God. Decide first which passage or thought in your study most powerfully moves you. Find one that challenges you to action, or causes you to want a closer relationship with God, or corrects a misconception about Him, or helps you respond to Him in a more satisfactory way.

a. Copy the verse or part of it:

> *"He is the beloved of the Lord and dwells beside Him securely. The Lord encircles him perpetually. . . " (Deuteronomy 33:12, MLB)*

b. Rewrite the verse in personalized form, using personal pronouns:

> *"I am the beloved of the Lord and I dwell beside Him securely. The Lord encircles me perpetually." (Deuteronomy 33:12, personalized)*

c. Make your own concise statement based on the verse or thought:

> *I am Your beloved child, Lord; You hold me securely in Your arms and encircle me at all times with loving protection.*

d. Choose a quote from someone else that touches your heart:

> *"Jesus, Lover of my soul, let me to Thy bosom fly, while the nearer waters roll, while the tempest still is nigh." (Charles Wesley)*

> *"Safety does not lie in the absence of danger but in the presence of the Lord."*

The object is to have *one* concise statement that moves you deeply in a positive way—one that meets a specific need or stimulates a better response to God, such as confidence, thankfulness, or desire. Because it is brief, you can quickly memorize it and meditate on it frequently.

Sometimes you will easily find your statement of truth because a passage captures your attention or meets an obvious need. At other times you will find it helpful to earnestly pray for truths that will help you in specific ways.

Perhaps you are frequently troubled by distressing emotions (resentment, anger, envy, anxiety, fear, self-condemnation, depression), or by disruptive outer responses to other people (angry outbursts, withdrawal, impatience, negativism, a critical spirit). Behind these obvious negative areas in your life you can often find false beliefs that trigger them. For example, you may consciously believe that God is reliable, but frequent anxieties may point to a hidden belief that He will fail you. Or behind your self-condemnation may be the hidden belief that Christ's sacrifice is not enough to assure forgiveness and that you must add an appropriate degree of self-punishment. Behind depression may be the belief that you are worthless or that you have no significant reason to live.

Seek to become aware of any hidden false beliefs behind your feelings and reactions, and find truths that will serve as antidotes to them. Pray frequently about this: "Lord, show me any false convictions that cause my negative emotions and reactions. And lead me to the scriptural truths that I can use again and again to counteract these false ideas and to produce in me positive emotions and responses to people."

Then be alert as you do these studies to find the statements of truth that you most need—statements through which God can further transform your thoughts and liberate you. When He gives you an appropriate statement, prayerfully go over it in your times alone with Him. Meditate on it until it grips your heart and stirs your imagination. Feed it into the depths of your mind frequently and with conviction.

Later, in your times of conscious need or failure, do three things. First, *acknowledge* what is happening in your thoughts, feelings, or reactions. Second, *choose against* being "pulled under" or led astray. Then consciously and emphatically *think* on your brief statement, thanking God that it is true. Keep meditating on it until the temptation passes or the need is met.

Finding and using statements of truth can be a key to increased liberation in your life, for Jesus promised, "You shall know the truth, and the truth shall make you free" (John 8:32).

6. Does someone near you—such as a friend, brother, sister, or spiritual child—have a need or problem that might be helped by some truth in this study? How can you help this person in [the topic being studied]?

In this section record the name of someone the Lord leads you to pray for and a tentative plan or key thoughts for helping that person.

When you share truths you have learned, be sensitive and loving; avoid a critical spirit or any hint of superiority. Often a tactful question or statement will open up a conversation: "Do you feel this might help you in your present disappointment?" or "I was wondering if this truth might overcome the fears you mentioned the other day."

Many times you can help others more effectively if you first share how *you* need this truth and how you want it to affect *your* life. Often this can lead into discussing the other person's needs also, and then praying for one another.

7. PRAY FOR FURTHER INSIGHTS or practical ideas that will help you grow in [the topic being studied]. Whenever you discover these, record them here for personal use and for sharing with others.

You can get these insights and ideas from various sources, such as your personal time with the Lord, your discussion of this study with others, or messages you hear. Recording your discoveries can prevent forgetting them as the years go by. They will increase your own involvement with God and your effectiveness with other people.

For some sample insights and ideas see the chart at the bottom of this page:

> *Much of our difficulty as seeking Christians stems from our unwillingness to take God as He is and adjust our lives accordingly. . . . As we go on to know Him better we shall find it a source of unspeakable joy that God is just what He is.*
>
> —A. W. TOZER*

---

*A. W. Tozer, *The Pursuit of God* (Harrisburg, Penn.: Christian Publications, Inc., 1948), p. 101.

FURTHER HELPS ON COMMUNING WITH HIM

Source	Insight or Idea
Bible study discussion group	*One of the men suggested we write out on several cards our brief statement of truth or the verse we like best and tape them for a week in places where we will see them often, such as the bathroom mirror, near a light switch, or on a closet door. I also decided to use one as a bookmark in my Bible or in a book I'm reading.*
Sunday morning sermon	*Our pastor suggested we use Philippians 2:13 as a prayer when our attitudes are wrong or when we face temptation: "Lord, right now, even though I don't feel like it, I give You permission to work in me both to will and to do of Your good pleasure, and I depend on You to do so." He said that this confirms his dependence on God and opens the way for God to work in him.*

NOTE: If you need more space to write, you'll find some extra space at the end of each chapter.

SEEKING
HIM

THE LORD IS IN your home. He is also in whatever room you withdraw to, making it the "secret place of His presence." Indeed, His presence extends from the highest heaven to the heavens that you see—and right down to where you are. You don't have to project your prayers through any ceiling or through space, for He's always right here, eager for you to seek Him. In a special way He's present with you in your quiet times and places, and best of all, He is *in* you through the indwelling of the Holy Spirit. You can slip into this inner refuge without making a move or blinking an eye and enjoy the calm of eternity.

Your loving Father, who is both with you in secret and exalted in heaven, is eager to act on your behalf. He will work *for* you in special ways as you seek Him— and even more important, He will work *in* you and *through* you.

Prayer

Lord, I open myself for You to penetrate the farthest depths of my being. I don't want my relationship with You to be shallow or reserved or confined by any limits I set, even unconsciously. I'm Yours—and I don't want to defend against You or any aspect of Your loving and working, at any level of my being.

Thank You for the privilege of seeking You and experiencing Your presence as I do this Bible study. Amen.

1. Verses to Consider: Psalms 34:8; 27:4; 42:1-2; Jeremiah 29:13; Isaiah 26:8-9; Philippians 3:7-10.

2. Favorite Passages: Copy from your Bible the verses or parts of verses that mean the most to you from the *Verses to Consider*. (In the future, add other Scriptures that speak to you in a definite way about seeking God. Use this part often for meditation and praise.)

3. Observations, Illustrations, and Quotations

4. How This Truth Can Affect My Life (Application)

5. Future Study

Extra space for writing answers:

NOTE: If you are able to spend more time on this topic, go on to the following pages. (Instructions are on pages 17-23.)

SEEKING HIM

Various men in the Scriptures made God the major pursuit of their lives and experienced an intimate relationship with Him. Others sought only His benefits and missed the richness of His intimate fellowship.

1. God called David a man after His own heart. As you read Psalm 63:1-5, what impresses you about David's desires and values and the results of these in his life?

2. In Psalm 73, Asaph went through a period of doubt as to the value of God's presence. After turning to God for insight, what conclusions did he reach about God and his relationship to Him, according to verses 25-28?

3. From the examples of Moses in Psalm 90:14 and David in Psalm 143:8, what can we learn about when to seek God and what to ask of Him?

4. Record what you find in Psalms 63:6-8, 119:164, and Daniel 6:10 about when to seek God and the attitudes to have as we approach Him.

The times and patterns men use in seeking God vary. One important consideration is to offer Him the best—to set aside a regular daily time that assures maximum alertness and minimum interruptions. Then we can supplement this with extra times such as an occasional half-day alone with Him and frequent refreshing pauses for praise, prayer, or meditation.

5. It is important to seek God in the Scriptures—meditating on His actual words rather than just our own impressions and thoughts. What do 1 Thessalonians 2:13, Hebrews 4:12, and 2 Timothy 3:16 tell us about why God's Word is so essential in our relating to Him?

6. The better we know God as He is revealed in the Scriptures and in His beloved Son, the more we will respond to His desire for involvement with us. Seeing His beauty, His strength, His victories, and His position can fill us with awe that *this* Person loves us and wants us to love Him. What descriptive phrases in Psalm 45:2-4 and Colossians 1:15-20 help you most to adore Him and want intimate fellowship with Him?

7. Select one passage from this study that motivates you to seek the Lord. Decide on a plan for using the verse you choose.

Extra space for writing answers:

DEPENDING ON HIM

D AY BY DAY, MOMENT by moment, we live physically by taking in air, water, and food. The air is all around us, ready for us to breathe it into our lungs. Food and water are there for us to eat and drink. In a similar way we live spiritually by simply taking in God. He is the One who gives us spiritual nourishment and energy. He is present and available, ready to meet our inner needs. He is around us and deep within us, eager for us to partake of Him through simple, quiet receptiveness. He is prepared to meet us more than halfway, always seeking to draw us into greater intimacy and dependence.

The amazing thing is not the occasional believer who constantly depends on the Lord with all his heart; the remarkable thing is that *all* of us do not depend on Him *all of the time*. Wholehearted trust is not a noble attainment, but the one sensible and appropriate response to such an awesome and faithful God.

Prayer

Thank You, Lord, for the constant reminders in Your Word of how dependent I am on You— reminders that destroy any illusion that I am independent and self-sufficient. Make me quickly aware when I get sidetracked, and draw me back to full dependence on You. May I enjoy Your peace instead of frustration, Your guidance instead of confusion, Your power instead of weakness.

Keep me tender to Your Word and dependent on Your Spirit in fresh ways as I do this Bible study. Amen.

1. Verses to Consider: Isaiah 50:10; Psalm 37:3-7; Proverbs 30:5; Zechariah 4:6; Philippians 4:13; Hebrews 4:16.

2. Favorite Passages: Copy from your Bible the verses or parts of verses that mean the most to you from the *Verses to Consider.* (In the future, add other Scriptures that speak to you in a definite way about depending on God. Use this part often for meditation and praise.)

3. Observations, Illustrations, and Quotations

4. How This Truth Can Affect My Life (Application)

5. Future Study

Extra space for writing answers:

NOTE: If you are able to spend more time on this topic, go on to the following pages. (Instructions are on pages 17-23.)

DEPENDING ON HIM

1. Look up the following verses. Meditate on them, then add the most meaningful portions to your *Favorite Passages*. As an option, find additional verses on your own.

   2 Chronicles 20:12-22; Jeremiah 17:5-8; Isaiah 40:27-31; Romans 4:20-21; 15:13; Psalm 31:19-20.

2. Write a paragraph or simple outline summarizing what your *Favorite Passages* (and possibly other verses you have considered) say about depending on God.

3. In your *Favorite Passages,* what truths stand out to you about God and His involvement with you, such as His attributes, His relationship to you, His attitudes, His desires, His promises, and His actions?

4. Answer one or both of the following:
   a. What thoughts, feelings, attitudes, or reservations have hindered me from depending on the Lord?

   b. Although my conscious mind may agree that depending on God is important, do my daily choices and actions demonstrate my belief? What changes in my schedule or in my manner of relating to God does He want me to make?

5. Write a brief statement about some truth that impresses you in this study, for frequent use in experiencing God's presence.

6. Does someone near you—such as a friend, brother, sister, or spiritual child—have a need or problem that might be helped by some truth in this study? How can you help this person desire to learn how to depend on God more fully?

7. Pray for further insights or practical ideas that will help you depend on God more completely. Whenever you discover something helpful, record it here for personal use and for sharing with others.

FURTHER HELPS ON DEPENDING ON GOD

Source	Insight or Idea

Extra space for writing answers:

COMMUNING
WITH HIM

OUR DELIGHTFUL INNER UNION with the Lord is for enabling us, so that we can be what He wants us to be and do what He wants us to do. But our union is also for intimacy, for a constant underlying sense of loving and being loved. And our union with Him is for communion. It makes possible a quiet inner retreat at any moment.

We need not draw away from the demands of life or escape to the mountains, though these things are great when possible and prudent. Wherever we are, we can taste and see that the Lord is good. We can hear His voice as we pause and tune in to a verse we have memorized. We can, so to speak, smell the fragrance of His garments: "All Thy garments are fragrant with myrrh and aloes and cassia" (Psalm 45:8). To do these things, we must let the Lord enlighten us more and more. We must develop our spiritual sensory organs through His Word and prayer and communion.

Prayer

Lord, through Your presence I have an inner place of peace, security, and rest that I can retreat to—a beautiful, tranquil sanctuary where I can find comfort and calm. You have poured out Your Spirit from on high to dwell in me and make Your presence more real to me. More and more, may I open up to You any wilderness areas in me—hidden or obvious—so that You will make them fertile fields where You can abide.

Work in me so that my times of quiet fellowship will be all You want them to be. And as I study this chapter, speak to me in special ways, leading me into richer and more constant communion with You. Amen.

1. Verses to Consider: Psalms 43:3-4; 36:7-8; Jeremiah 15:16; Luke 24:32; Psalms 23:1-6; 27:8.

2. Favorite Passages: Copy from your Bible the verses or parts of verses that mean the most to you from the *Verses to Consider.* (In the future, add other Scriptures that speak to you in a definite way about communing with God. Use this part often for meditation and praise.)

3. Observations, Illustrations, and Quotations

4. How This Truth Can Affect My Life (Application)

5. Future Study

Extra space for writing answers:

NOTE: If you are able to spend more time on this topic, go on to the following pages. (Instructions are on pages 17-23.)

CHAP. 3 / CONTINUED
COMMUNING WITH HIM

1. Look up the following verses. Meditate on them and then add the most meaningful portions to your *Favorite Passages*. As an option, find additional verses on your own.

   Psalm 90:14; Revelation 3:20; 1 John 1:3-5; Proverbs 3:32; 1 Corinthians 1:9.

2. Write a paragraph or simple outline summarizing what your *Favorite Passages* (and possibly other verses you have considered) say about communing with God.

3. In your *Favorite Passages,* what truths stand out to you about God and His involvement with you, such as His attributes, His relationship to you, His attitudes, His desires, His promises, and His actions?

4. Answer one or both of the following:
   a. What thoughts, feelings, attitudes, or reservations have hindered me from communing with the Lord?

   b. Although my conscious mind may agree that communing with God is important, do my daily choices and actions demonstrate my belief? What changes in my schedule or in my manner of relating to God does He want me to make?

5. Write a brief statement about some truth that impresses you in this study, for frequent use in experiencing God's presence.

6. Does someone near you—such as a friend, brother, sister, or spiritual child—have a need or problem that might be helped by some truth in this study? How can you help this person desire or learn how to commune with God more effectively?

7. Pray for further insights or practical ideas that will help you commune with God in a richer way. Whenever you discover something helpful, record it here for personal use and for sharing with others.

FURTHER HELPS ON COMMUNING WITH GOD

Source	Insight or Idea

Extra space for writing answers:

LISTENING
TO HIS WORD

TO TRULY RECEIVE the Lord's Word is to receive in a fuller way Him who is Life. Through His Word He nurtures and nourishes us; He gives us Himself. This opens the way to enjoying His love, His guidance, His grace, and His power to obey. As George Mueller wrote, "The vigor of our spiritual life will be in exact proportion to the place held by the Bible in our life and thoughts."

How wonderful it is to have God's Word! It is our guidebook for effective living, our handbook for wise decision-making, our compass for navigating through life, our ultimate source of encouragement and inspiration. Most of all, it is our window through which we can glimpse the very heart of God.

Prayer

Thank You, Lord, for Your authentic, tested, utterly reliable Word. It opens my eyes to the unseen world—to the invisible realities that are infinitely more enduring and delightful than anything in the physical world. What a joy to come to Your Word and let You show me Your treasures, Your glorious purposes, and most of all, the wonders of who You are.

Now as I meditate on the Scriptures in this study, I draw near to You and listen to what You are saying through them. I count on You to draw near to me, making this a time of rich fellowship with You. Amen.

1. Verses to Consider: Matthew 11:28-29; 1 Corinthians 2:12-13; Proverbs 2:1-6; 8:34; Psalm 25:5,8-10,14; Luke 10:38-42.

2. Favorite Passages: Copy from your Bible the verses or parts of verses that mean the most to you from the *Verses to Consider*. (In the future, add other Scriptures that speak to you in a definite way about listening to God's Word. Use this part often for meditation and praise.)

3. Observations, Illustrations, and Quotations

4. How This Truth Can Affect My Life (Application)

5. Future Study

Extra space for writing answers:

NOTE: If you are able to spend more time on this topic, go on to the following pages. (Instructions are on pages 17-23.)

CHAP. 4 / CONTINUED
LISTENING TO HIS WORD

1. Look up the following verses. Meditate on them and then add the most meaningful portions to your *Favorite Passages.* As an option, find additional verses on your own.

   John 8:31-32; Proverbs 22:17-21; John 17:6-8,13; 2 Peter 1:2-4; Psalm 139:17-18; John 15:11; 16:33.

2. Write a paragraph or simple outline summarizing what your *Favorite Passages* (and possibly other verses you have considered) say about listening to God's Word.

3. In your *Favorite Passages,* what truths stand out to you about God and His involvement with you, such as His attributes, His relationship to you, His attitudes, His desires, His promises, and His actions?

4. Answer one or both of the following:
   a. What thoughts, feelings, attitudes, or reservations have hindered me from listening to God's Word?

   b. Although my conscious mind may agree that listening to God's Word is important, do my daily choices and actions demonstrate my belief? What changes in my schedule or in my manner of relating to God does He want me to make?

5. Write a brief statement about some truth that impresses you in this study, for frequent use in experiencing God's presence.

6. Does someone near you—such as a friend, brother, sister, or spiritual child—have a need or problem that might be helped by some truth in this study? How can you help this person desire or learn how to listen to God more effectively?

7. Pray for further insights or practical ideas that will help you listen to God's Word with greater profit. Whenever you discover something helpful, record it here for personal use and for sharing with others.

FURTHER HELPS ON LISTENING TO GOD'S WORD

SOURCE	INSIGHT OR IDEA

Extra space for writing answers:

CONFIDING
IN HIM

ISN'T IT AMAZING THAT GOD, the Ruler of all things everywhere, takes delight in hearing our prayers? He wants us to pour out to Him our needs and feelings in detailed, thankful prayer. Yet at times we may recount the details of our concerns but forget to express gratitude. Do we forget to give thanks that He allows trials to come into our lives to refine us, that He promises to work for us, and that He will do so? Sometimes it helps to tell Him all the particulars about a specific need, ask Him to work in His way and time, and then concentrate on thanksgiving. We can focus on the positive things we want Him do to rather than reviewing time and again the painful details.

If your heart is deeply concerned about a prolonged problem, you need not review the grim details day after day. Instead, write down one or more positives that you would like the Lord to do—positives that would overcome the negatives. Then keep on asking for those positives with confidence and thanksgiving.

Prayer

Lord, how I love to know that You hear me! Indeed, You long for me to con-
fide in You. I'm so grateful that You are always available, welcoming and
attentive. Thank You that I can depend on You with never a fear that I'm
imposing. Work in me, Lord, a greater consistency in bringing my requests to
You with thanksgiving.

As I study these Scriptures, open my heart to trust You more fully and
confide in You more deeply as the days and weeks go by. Amen.

1. Verses to Consider: Psalm 62:8; Philippians 4:6-7; Hebrews 4:14-16; Psalms 102:1-7; 55:22; Proverbs 16:3.

2. Favorite Passages: Copy from your Bible the verses or parts of verses that mean the most to you from the *Verses to Consider*. (In the future, add other Scriptures that speak to you in a definite way about confiding in God. Use this part often for meditation and praise.)

3. Observations, Illustrations, and Quotations

4. How This Truth Can Affect My Life (Application)

5. Future Study

Extra space for writing answers:

NOTE: If you are able to spend more time on this topic, go on to the following pages. (Instructions are on pages 17-23.)

CHAP. 5 / CONTINUED
CONFIDING IN HIM

1. Look up the following verses. Meditate on them and then add the most meaningful portions to your *Favorite Passages*. As an option, find additional verses on your own.

   Psalm 100:1-2; Matthew 6:6-7; Romans 8:26; 2 Chronicles 14:11; Psalms 34:4-6; 116:1-2.

2. Write a paragraph or simple outline summarizing what your *Favorite Passages* (and possibly other verses you have considered) say about confiding in God.

3. In your *Favorite Passages,* what truths stand out to you about God and His involvement with you, such as His attributes, His relationship to you, His attitudes, His desires, His promises, and His actions?

4. Answer one or both of the following:
   a. What thoughts, feelings, attitudes, or reservations have hindered me from confiding in the Lord?

   b. Although my conscious mind may agree that confiding in God is important, do my daily choices and actions demonstrate my belief? What changes in my schedule or in my manner of relating to God does He want me to make?

5. Write a brief statement about some truth that impresses you in this study, for frequent use in experiencing God's presence.

6. Does someone near you—such as a friend, brother, sister, or spiritual child—have a need or problem that might be helped by some truth in this study? How can you help this person desire or learn how to confide in God more fully?

7. Pray for further insights or practical ideas that will help you confide in God more. Whenever you discover something helpful, record it here for personal use and for sharing with others.

FURTHER HELPS ON CONFIDING IN GOD

Source	Insight or Idea

Extra space for writing answers:

—DWELLING IN HIM— AND HE IN ME

GOD WANTS TO FILL US with His loving, liberating presence. He dispels the "negatives" in our lives with His love, joy, and peace. He subdues the destructive influence of Satan and the flesh. When He fills us, He liberates our wills to choose what we *really* want.

Christ dwelling in us and we in Him forms a living union deep inside us. We can settle down in a deepening relationship and live our lives from that inner home. Yet it's not a matter of "going in and out" as we do in a home made of wood and stone. We can coexist within the sanctuary of our spiritual life *and* out in the world, with its problems and perils. It's being in and out at the same time, for we have an inner fountain that springs up in us with fresh life and flows out into our relationships, duties, and trials.

Prayer

Thank You, Father, that You have placed me in Christ. You have welcomed me into Him and united me with Him, making Him the Life of my life. You have turned my human spirit into a sanctuary where He lives now and forever. What mercy! What love and grace! I rejoice that, by this union, You have recreated me in my innermost being. You have made me a new creation, a new person, with a whole new source of life—a new inner spring from which life flows.

As study dwelling in You and You in me, give me fresh understanding of each Scripture I ponder. Amen.

1. Verses to Consider: Isaiah 57:15; John 14:23; 1 Corinthians 6:19-20; Philippians 2:13; Colossians 1:27; 2 Corinthians 6:16.

2. Favorite Passages: Copy from your Bible the verse or parts of verses that mean the most to you from the *Verses to Consider*. (In the future, add other Scriptures that speak to you in a definite way about dwelling in God and His dwelling in you. Use this part often for meditation and praise.)

3. Observations, Illustrations, and Quotations

4. How This Truth Can Affect My Life (Application)

5. Future Study

Extra space for writing answers:

NOTE: If you are able to spend more time on this topic, go on to the following pages. (Instructions are on pages 17-23.)

CHAP. 6 / CONTINUED
DWELLING IN HIM—AND HE IN ME

1. Look up the following verses. Meditate on them and then add the most meaningful portions to your *Favorite Passages.* As an option, find additional verses on your own.

   Ephesians 3:16-19; John 15:5,9; 1 John 2:28; 4:16; Psalm 91:1-2; Deuteronomy 33:12.

2. Write a paragraph or simple outline summarizing what your *Favorite Passages* (and possibly other verses you have considered) say about dwelling in God and His dwelling in you.

3. In your *Favorite Passages,* what truths stand out to you about God and His involvement with you, such as His attributes, His relationship to you, His attitudes, His desires, His promises, and His actions?

4. Answer one or both of the following:
   a. What thoughts, feelings, attitudes, or reservations have hindered me from dwelling in the Lord and allowing Him to dwell in me?

   b. Although my conscious mind may agree that my dwelling in God and His dwelling in me are important, do my daily choices and actions demonstrate my belief? What changes in my schedule or in my manner of relating to God does He want me to make?

5. Write a brief statement about some truth that impresses you in this study for frequent use in experiencing God's presence.

6. Does someone near you—such as a friend, brother, sister, or spiritual child—have a need or problem that might be helped by some truth in this study? How can you help this person desire or learn how to dwell in God more fully?

7. Pray for further insights or practical ideas that will help you dwell in God and allow Him to dwell in you more fully and more constantly. Whenever you discover something helpful, record it here for personal use and for sharing with others.

FURTHER HELPS ON DWELLING IN GOD—AND HE IN ME

SOURCE	INSIGHT OR IDEA

Extra space for writing answers:

WALKING WITH HIM

I F YOU'VE EVER TAKEN a trip to an unfamiliar land, you know how reassuring it is to have an experienced guide with you to show the way. If you've ever embarked on a strenuous journey—a cross-country trek or an overseas missions trip—you know how comforting it is to have a traveling companion who is optimistic and cheerful.

This is the high privilege we have with the Lord as our Guide, Encourager, and all-powerful Protector for our journey here on earth. He will always be with us to show us the way, to bear our burdens, to provide us with inner and outer strength, to keep us on the right path, and to give us countless delights and constant reassurance all along the way. We can take great solace in our Father's promise: "I, the Lord your God, will hold your right hand, whispering to you, 'Do not fear, I will help you'" (Isaiah 41:13).

Prayer

Thank You, Lord, for the privilege of walking through life with You. Thank You that moment by moment I can enjoy Your presence and depend on You for renewed strength. I rejoice that with You I can run and not grow weary, I can walk and not faint. And I thank You that all along the way, You are preparing me for our ultimate destination, coaching me on the customs and culture of our eternal home.

As I study the Scriptures on walking with You, open wide the eyes of my heart to see how I should live and assure me of how sufficient you are to guide me all the way to my heavenly home. Amen.

1. Verses to Consider: Joshua 1:9; Micah 6:8; Psalms 23:4; 73:21-24,28; Malachi 2:6.

2. Favorite Passages: Copy from your Bible the verses or parts of verses that mean the most to you from the *Verses to Consider*. (In the future, add other Scriptures that speak to you in a definite way about walking with God. Use this part often for meditation and praise.)

3. Observations, Illustrations, and Quotations

4. How This Truth Can Affect My Life (Application)

5. Future Study

Extra space for writing answers:

NOTE: If you are able to spend more time on this topic, go on to the following pages. (Instructions are on pages 17-23.)

CHAP. 7 / CONTINUED
WALKING WITH HIM

1. Look up the following verses. Meditate on them and then add the most meaningful portions to your *Favorite Passages.* As an option, find additional verses on your own.

   Hebrews 13:5-6; 2 Chronicles 32:7-8; Isaiah 43:2; 1 Thessalonians 4:1-2; Galatians 5:16; Ephesians 5:2.

2. Write a paragraph or simple outline summarizing what your *Favorite Passages* (and possibly other verses you have considered) say about walking with God.

3. In your *Favorite Passages,* what truths stand out to you about God and His involvement with you, such as His attributes, His relationship to you, His attitudes, His desires, His promises, and His actions?

4. Answer one or both of the following:
   a. What thoughts, feelings, attitudes, or reservations have hindered me from walking with the Lord?

   b. Although my conscious mind may agree that walking with God is important, do my daily choices and actions demonstrate my belief? What changes in my schedule or in my manner of relating to God does He want me to make?

5. Write a brief statement about some truth that impresses you in this study for frequent use in experiencing God's presence.

6. Does someone near you—such as a friend, brother, sister, or spiritual child—have a need or problem that might be helped by some truth in this study? How can you help this person desire or learn how to walk with God more closely?

7. Pray for further insights or practical ideas that will help you walk with God more closely. Whenever you discover something helpful, record it here for personal use and for sharing with others.

FURTHER HELPS ON WALKING WITH GOD

SOURCE	INSIGHT OR IDEA

Extra space for writing answers:

OBEYING
HIM

O N THE SURFACE, GOD'S commands may seem difficult, demanding, perhaps even impossible. But someone once said, "God's commands are always opportunities in disguise." The Lord's directives carry with them His enabling, which comes as we choose to trust and obey. As we read the "fine print" and understand the context of God's instructions, we find that His commands are invitations, opportunities, and safeguards.

We can and should make plans for the future; we should dream our dreams and think of what we would like to do for God. But we must settle our hearts before Him, content to obey His leading and calling. We bring the Lord joy by longing to do what we feel will glorify Him—and then being content to leave some of it undone if that is what He desires.

Prayer

A wonderful prayer to attune your heart to God's leading and lordship comes from Henrietta Mears, who began each day by saying something like this:

Lord, here are my feet to take me where You want today. Here is my body to live for You today. Here are my hands to serve You. Here are my eyes to see what You want and only what You want. Here are my ears to hear what You desire. Here is my mouth to speak only what pleases You. Here is my mind to think Your thoughts and guide me in my actions all day long.

Thank You, Lord, for the privilege of obeying You, the most gracious and wise of all commanders. I pray that You will use this study to make my obedience to You more total and more enjoyable. Amen.

1. Verses to Consider: Luke 6:46-49; Deuteronomy 5:29; James 1:22-25; Psalm 119:9-11,59-60; Luke 8:21; Romans 12:1-2.

2. Favorite Passages: Copy from your Bible the verses or parts of verses that mean the most to you from the *Verses to Consider*. (In the future, add other Scriptures that speak to you in a definite way about obeying God. Use this part often for meditation and praise.)

3. Observations, Illustrations, and Quotations

4. How This Truth Can Affect My Life (Application)

5. Future Study

Extra space for writing answers:

NOTE: If you are able to spend more time on this topic, go on to the following pages. (Instructions are on pages 17-23.)

CHAP. 8 / CONTINUED
OBEYING HIM

1. From the passages listed in *Verses to Consider,* list some reasons why God longs for you to obey Him.

2. What does God desire in your heart response and your actions so He can increasingly demonstrate His love and presence to you? (see John 14:21-24; Deuteronomy 7:9).

3. Write a paragraph explaining and personally applying the "great commandments" (see Matthew 22:36-40).

4. Like rays shining from the sun, God's desire to be involved with us is constant. But we can turn our back to Him and experience night instead of light, desolation instead of warm fellowship. Consider Isaiah 59:1-2 and Psalm 32:5 and record here the cause and cure of broken fellowship.

In no way do we earn God's love by obeying Him; rather, we merely choose the one path where God's love shines undimmed and where He promises to manifest His presence and enrich our lives. On that path, we keep ourselves in the center of God's love and blessing. There we "let Him love us."

5. When you feel that something is blocking out the warmth of God's love but are not aware of any sin in your life, what should you do? (See Psalms 139:23-24; 119:130; Hebrews 4:12-13.)

6. To help restore your sense of God's loving presence after confession, envision the Lord treating you like the father treated the son in Luke 15:11-32. Describe the father's feelings and reactions, and then the son's. If the father had been cold and legalistic, what might he have said? Instead, what did he do immediately after the son confessed?

7. From Hebrews 11:24-27, what do you learn about the keys to obedience and the cost of obedience?

8. Consider Philippians 2:13 and 1 John 5:4-5. In regard to obedience and victory, what do you discover about God's part and our part?

SERVING
HIM

PEOPLE CAN MAKE IMITATION fruit out of many different materials—plastic, wax, wood, glass, and crystal. But no one can manufacture real fruit, and we certainly can't make spiritual fruit. The only way we can bear spiritual fruit is when the "soil" of our lives is watered by the Spirit, nourished by God's Word, and tended by His loving hands. As our roots become firmly established in God, we find ourselves growing, flourishing, and fulfilling the purpose to which He calls us. Then those around us benefit from the outgrowth of the Spirit's work within us.

We would do well to echo the words of Benjamin Jenks (1646-1724). Here is his prayer in contemporary English: "O Lord, renew our spirits and draw our hearts to You so that our work may not be to us a burden, but a delight; and give us a mighty love for You that will sweeten all our obedience. Oh, let us not serve You with the spirit of bondage as slaves, but with the cheerfulness and gladness of children, delighting ourselves in You and rejoicing in Your work."

Prayer

Lord, I pause before You, my gracious King, for You are also the Judge who will reward me according to how I live and serve You. I pause not to scrutinize how well I've been doing, but to pray that You will enable me to labor earnestly for abiding fruit. May I not labor in vain. May I bear fruit that is the outflow of Your life in me.

Father, as I study these Scriptures, prepare me more fully for the ways You want me to serve You, both now and in the future. Amen.

1. Verses to Consider: Matthew 9:36-38; 2 Corinthians 5:14-15,18-20; Matthew 28:19-20; Galatians 6:9-10; 2 Corinthians 9:6-9; Matthew 25:34-40.

2. Favorite Passages: Copy from your Bible the verses or parts of verses that mean the most to you from the *Verses to Consider.* (In the future, add other Scriptures that speak to you in a definite way about serving God. Use this part often for meditation and praise.)

3. Observations, Illustrations, and Quotations

4. How This Truth Can Affect My Life (Application)

5. Future Study

Extra space for writing answers:

_____

NOTE: If you are able to spend more time on this topic, go on to the following pages. (Instructions are on pages 17-23.)

CHAP. 9 / CONTINUED

SERVING HIM

1. Look up the following verses. Meditate on them, then add the most meaningful portions to your *Favorite Passages*. As an option, find additional verses on your own.

   Ephesians 6:18-19; Colossians 1:28-29; Romans 14:19; 12:4-8; Hebrews 6:10; Isaiah 58:6-12

2. Write a paragraph or simple outline summarizing what your *Favorite Passages* (and possibly other verses you have considered) say about serving God.

3. In your *Favorite Passages,* what truths stand out to you about God and His involvement with you, such as His attributes, His relationship to you, His attitudes, His desires, His promises, and His actions?

4. Answer one or both of the following:

   a. What thoughts, feelings, attitudes, or reservations have hindered me from serving the Lord?

   b. Although my conscious mind may agree that serving God is important, do my daily choices and actions demonstrate my belief? What changes in my schedule or in my manner of relating to God does He want me to make?

5. Write a brief statement about some truth that impresses you in this study for frequent use in experiencing God's presence.

6. Does someone near you—such as a friend, brother, sister, or spiritual child—have a need or problem that might be helped by some truth in this study? How can you help this person desire or learn how to serve God more effectively?

7. Pray for further insights or practical ideas that will help you serve God more effectively. Whenever you discover something helpful, record it here for personal use and for sharing with others.

FURTHER HELPS ON SERVING GOD

SOURCE	INSIGHT OR IDEA

Extra space for writing answers:

ENJOYING
HIS SUPPORT

A. W. TOZER ONCE said, "The fellowship of God is delightful beyond all telling. He communes with His redeemed ones in an easy, uninhibited fellowship that is restful and healing to the soul. . . . He loves us for ourselves and values our love more than galaxies of new created worlds."[1]

Do you have a special mental scene that you can retreat to for inner refreshment and fellowship with God? Perhaps you envision being sheltered in the shadow of His wings, curling up by a cozy fireplace, relaxing in a peaceful church sanctuary, or absorbing the beauty of a sunset or a starry sky. Choose your favorite inner getaway and read the following prayer.

Prayer

Dear Lord, as I quietly pause before You, may I feel Your touch of love and strength and power. I open myself to You and Your boundless love that is upholding me, surrounding me, and overshadowing me. I open myself to let Your Spirit flood my heart like warm spring sunlight. Breathe into me a fresh sense of Your kindness and goodness, and fill me with Your wisdom. What a privilege it is to tap into Your depths of understanding and see things from Your eternal perspective.

Father, as I meditate on the Scriptures in this study, create in my mind and spirit a joyful sense of who You are and a growing trust in what You promise to do for me. Amen.

---

1. A. W. Tozer, *Whatever Happened to Worship?* (Camp Hill, Penn.: Christian Publications, 1985), pp. 25-26.

1. Verses to Consider: Psalms 94:18-19; 18:35-36; Deuteronomy 33:27; Isaiah 41:13-14; Daniel 10:18-19; Psalm 37:23-24.

2. Favorite Passages: Copy from your Bible the verses or parts of verses that mean the most to you from the *Verses to Consider.* (In the future, add other Scriptures that speak to you in a definite way about enjoying God's support. Use this part often for meditation and praise.)

3. Observations, Illustrations, and Quotations

4. How This Truth Can Affect My Life (Application)

5. Future Study

Extra space for writing answers:

NOTE: If you are able to spend more time on this topic, go on to the following pages. (Instructions are on pages 17-23.)

CHAP. 10 / CONTINUED
ENJOYING HIS SUPPORT

1. Look up the following verses. Meditate on them and then add the most meaningful portions to your *Favorite Passages.* As an option, find additional verses on your own.

   Psalm 44:3; Isaiah 46:3-4; Hosea 11:3-4; Luke 15:20; Psalms 57:1-2; 63:7-8.

2. Write a paragraph or simple outline summarizing what your *Favorite Passages* (and possibly other verses you have considered) say about enjoying God's support.

3. In your *Favorite Passages,* what truths stand out to you about God and His involvement with you, such as His attributes, His relationship to you, His attitudes, His desires, His promises, and His actions?

4. Answer one or both of the following:

a. What thoughts, feelings, attitudes, or reservations have hindered me from enjoying the Lord's support?

b. Although my conscious mind may agree that enjoying God's support is important, do my daily choices and actions demonstrate my belief? What changes in my schedule or in my manner of relating to God does He want me to make?

5. Write a brief statement about some truth that impresses you in this study for frequent use in experiencing God's presence.

6. Does someone near you—such as a friend, brother, sister, or spiritual child—have a need or problem that might be helped by some truth in this study? How can you help this person desire or learn how to enjoy God's support more?

7. Pray for further insights or practical ideas that will help you enjoy more fully God's support. Whenever you discover something helpful, record it here, for personal use and for sharing with others.

FURTHER HELPS ON ENJOYING GOD'S SUPPORT

Source	Insight or Idea

Extra space for writing answers:

MAINTAINING FELLOWSHIP WITH HIS PEOPLE

TO ENJOY THE FULLEST possible relationship with God, we must also relate to His family. As the Bible tells us, "If we love one another, God abides in us, and His love is perfected in us" (1 John 4:12).

Do we want to live with no cloud hiding the face of the Father, with no smog in our spiritual atmosphere? Do we want an unhindered, growing experience of Him and what He is to us? Or do we want the miserable luxury of hard feelings against a brother or sister in the Lord's family? Let's keep in mind that when Christians argue or quarrel, Satan supplies ammunition to both sides. So instead of pleasing Satan, let's humbly pray for the faults of others and praise the Lord for their virtues. And let's remember to praise and commend those for whom we're praying.

Prayer

Today, dear Lord, may I look with love and respect on every person I meet— believer or unbeliever—and relate to each one with gentle wisdom. May I see beyond the flaws and faults of Your children to that which is good and praiseworthy. May I fill my mind with appreciation and gratitude, not with complaints and grievances. If you call me to correct or admonish someone, may I speak the truth in a timely way with gracious love. Silence my lips to all unkind words and fill them with words of encouragement.

As I meditate on the Scriptures in this study, show me fresh ways to live in fellowship with Your people. Amen.

1. Verses to Consider: Hebrews 10:24-25; Philippians 2:1-4; Ephesians 4:1-3,32; Matthew 5:23-24; Galatians 6:1-2; Romans 15:5-7.

2. Favorite Passages: Copy from your Bible the verses or parts of verses that mean the most to you from the *Verses to Consider.* (In the future, add other Scriptures that speak to you in a definite way about maintaining fellowship with God's people. Use this part often for meditation and praise.)

3. Observations, Illustrations, and Quotations

4. How This Truth Can Affect My Life (Application)

5. Future Study

Extra space for writing answers:

NOTE: If you are able to spend more time on this topic, go on to the following pages. (Instructions are on pages 17-23.)

MAINTAINING FELLOWSHIP WITH HIS PEOPLE

1. Look up the following verses. Meditate on them, then add the most meaningful portions to your *Favorite Passages*. As an option, find additional verses on your own.

   Colossians 3:16; Ephesians 4:11-12,15-16; 1 John 1:5-7; Malachi 3:16; Ephesians 2:19-22; Psalm 34:1-3

2. Write a paragraph or simple outline summarizing what your *Favorite Passages* (and possibly other verses you have considered) say about maintaining fellowship with God's people.

3. In your *Favorite Passages,* what truths stand out to you about God and His involvement with you, such as His attributes, His relationship to you, His attitudes, His desires, His promises, and His actions?

4. Answer one or both of the following:
   a. What thoughts, feelings, attitudes, or reservations have hindered me from maintaining fellowship with the Lord's people?

   b. Although my conscious mind may agree that maintaining fellowship with God's people is important, do my daily choices and actions demonstrate my belief? What changes in my schedule or in my manner of relating to God's people does He want me to make?

5. Write a brief statement about some truth that impresses you in this study for frequent use in experiencing God's presence.

6. Does someone near you—such as a friend, brother, sister, or spiritual child—have a need or problem that might be helped by some truth in this study? How can you help this person desire or learn how to maintain fellowship with God's people more regularly and effectively?

7. Pray for further insights or practical ideas that will help you maintain unified and edifying fellowship with God's people. Whenever you discover something helpful, record it here for personal use and for sharing with others.

FURTHER HELPS ON MAINTAINING FELLOWSHIP WITH GOD'S PEOPLE

Source	Insight or Idea

Extra space for writing answers:

DELIGHTING IN HIM

WHEN EARTHLY DELIGHTS CAUSE our hearts to shout for joy, we can let that wonderful feeling spill over into worship of God. He wants us to enjoy life's goodness and celebrate His creativity. And when we encounter trials and disappointments, He wants us to experience His love and strength, which undergird us through all our hardships.

Our heavenly Father has given us many wonders to delight in—and none is more wonderful than Himself!

Prayer

Lord, I find my deepest joy and satisfaction not in what I can accomplish or achieve, but in You—simply in being in Your presence. I long for greater constancy in my relating to You. I want Christ to feel at home in my heart at all times, unhindered by anything. I want a wide-open inner response of love for You, a readiness for You to expand within me, stretching out new spaces in my heart for You to fill.

Now, Father, as I do this study, open my eyes that I may behold wondrous things in Your Word—especially the wondrous things about You. Amen.

1. Verses to Consider: Isaiah 61:10; Psalm 84:1-4; 1 Peter 1:8; Romans 5:11; Psalm 18:1-3.

2. Favorite Passages: Copy from your Bible the verses or parts of verses that mean the most to you from the *Verses to Consider.* (In the future, add other Scriptures that speak to you in a definite way about delighting in God. Use this part often for meditation and praise.)

3. Observations, Illustrations, and Quotations

4. How This Truth Can Affect My Life (Application)

5. Future Study

Extra space for writing answers:

NOTE: If you are able to spend more time on this topic, go on to the following pages. (Instructions are on pages 17-23.)

CHAP. 12 / CONTINUED
DELIGHTING IN HIM

1. Look up the following verses. Meditate on them and then add the most meaningful portions to your *Favorite Passages.* As an option, find additional verses on your own.

   Luke 1:46-47; Psalms 16:5-9,11; 126:2-3; Habakkuk 3:17-18; Revelation 15:3-4.

2. Write a paragraph or simple outline summarizing what your *Favorite Passages* (and possibly other verses you have considered) say about delighting in God.

3. In your *Favorite Passages,* what truths stand out to you about God and His involvement with you, such as His attributes, His relationship to you, His attitudes, His desires, His promises, and His actions?

4. Answer one or both of the following:

a. What thoughts, feelings, attitudes, or reservations have hindered me from delighting in the Lord?

b. Although my conscious mind may agree that delighting in God is important, do my daily choices and actions demonstrate my belief? What changes in my schedule or in my manner of relating to God does He want me to make?

5. Write a brief statement about some truth that impresses you in this study for frequent use in experiencing God's presence.

6. Does someone near you—such as a friend, brother, sister, or spiritual child—have a need or problem that might be helped by some truth in this study? How can you help this person desire or learn how to delight in God more fully?

7. Pray for further insights or practical ideas that will help you delight in God more. Whenever you discover something helpful, record it here for personal use and for sharing with others.

FURTHER HELPS ON DELIGHTING IN GOD

Source	Insight or Idea

Extra space for writing answers:

REVIEWING
GOD'S PRESENCE

THIS STUDY GIVES YOU the opportunity to review God's presence with you and the ways in which He wants you to become more involved with Him.

Prayer

Lord, I turn my heart over to You. I center my mind and my emotions on You with a quiet withdrawing from all distractions. You know the troubles and trials, the pain and pressures that often surround me. You know the ways I tend to let these concerns dictate my thoughts and feelings, blocking the flow of Your loving sufficiency within me. So I settle into Your holy presence within me, into Your sanctuary of love. I bring my entire being into restful, refreshing fellowship with You.

Now, Lord, guide my thoughts as I review the chapters of this study book, and deeply enrich my experience of Your presence in my life. Lead me to the truths You especially want me to focus on, now and in the future. Amen.

1. Prayerfully review your *Favorite Passages* in the preceding studies. Then record in each following category several passages that are especially meaningful to you.

   a. God's character and attributes—your admiration for Him

b. God's involvement and attitudes—your importance to Him

c. God's invitations and commands—your involvement with Him

2. Copy one or two of your *Favorite Passages* that have most influenced you toward fuller involvement with God.

3. Which application (part 5) from your twelve studies do you most want to pray about further and use in the coming weeks? Or is God laying a new application on your heart?

4. Is there any particular area of your life that you want to dedicate to God in view of what He is to you? Anything in respect to your priorities, your relationships, your longings, your future plans? Or your entire self? Have you made Him Lord of all? Consider each of these questions prayerfully, allowing time for God to speak to your heart.

5. Record here—or in question 4 of each study—further observations or illustrations that come to mind on any of the topics.

NOTE: If you are able to spend more time on this topic, go on to the following pages. (Instructions are on pages 17-23.)

CHAP. 13 / CONTINUED
REVIEWING GOD'S PRESENCE

1. Review your summaries (question 2 in your additional studies) and write a paragraph or outline summarizing what you have learned about experiencing God's presence.

2. Review question 5 in your additional studies and copy here the one "statement of truth" that you most want to remember and use.

3. As you think back over the topics you have studied, write a statement or brief paragraph on how these studies have helped you overcome misconceptions of God, fears about Him, or feelings against Him.

4. As a result of having studied these topics, what has God done for you in demonstrating His love, satisfying your mind or heart, or changing your thoughts or feelings about yourself? Record one or two highlights here.

5. Consider writing a letter to a friend or young Christian, sharing something that stood out to you in this review. Also consider asking that person to pray as you apply that truth to a particular need in your life. Write down names of people to whom you might write and a short statement of what you would share.

But simply to drop all our dreams and ambitions and preferences and have no mind about it at all, but be willing for God to shift us anywhere on life's checkerboard, or bury us anywhere in life's garden, counting not our lives dear and loving them not unto death, gladly yielding ourselves for God to please Himself with, anywhere and anyway He chooses—that is rarely done.

—Anonymous

Purge me, Lord, of my follies;
An empty cup let me be,
Waiting only Thy filling,
Hungry only for Thee.

Can even the Lord pour blessing
Into a cup that is full?
Put treasure into a locked hand
Be He ever so bountiful?

Empty me, Lord, and make me
Hungry only for Thee.
Only Thy bread once tasted
Can ever satisfy me.

—Author unknown

If any man thirst, let him come unto Me and drink (John 7:37). Who does not thirst? Who has not mind-thirsts or heart-thirsts, soul-thirsts or body thirsts? Well, no matter which, or whether I have them all, "Come unto me"—and remain thirsty? Ah no! "Come unto Me and drink."

What, can Jesus meet my need? Yes, and more than meet it. No matter how intricate my path, how difficult my service; no matter how sad my bereavement, how far away my loved ones; no matter how helpless I am, how deep are my soul-yearnings—Jesus can meet all, all and more than meet.

—J. Hudson Taylor[1]

That God desires our fellowship is, perhaps, one of the most amazing facts conveyed to us through the Scriptures. This fact is so staggering in its conception that it is extremely difficult for us fully to grasp and consider its significance.

That God should allow His creatures to have fellowship with Himself is wonderful enough; but that He can desire *it, that it gives Him satisfaction and joy and pleasure, is almost too much for understanding.*

—The Quiet Time[2]

---

1. As quoted in *Hudson Taylor's Spiritual Secret* by Dr. and Mrs. Howard Taylor (Philadelphia: China Inland Mission, 1958), p. 122.

2. *The Quiet Time* by the InterVarsity Christian Fellowship (Downers Grove, Ill.: InterVarsity Press, 1945), p. 2.

FOR FURTHER READING

THE FOLLOWING ARE SOME excellent books and booklets on having a dynamic relationship with God:

Demarest, Bruce. *Satisfy Your Soul* (Colorado Springs, Colo.: NavPress, 1999).

Foster, Robert D. *Seven Minutes with God—How to Plan a Daily Quiet Time* (pamphlet, 1954).

Mayhall, Carole. *When God Whispers* (Colorado Springs, Colo.: NavPress, 1997).

Munger, Robert Boyd. *My Heart—Christ's Home* (Downers Grove, Ill.: InterVarsity, 2001).

Packer, James I. *Knowing God* (Downers Grove, Ill.: InterVarsity, 1993).

Taylor, J. Hudson. *Union and Communion* (Minneapolis, Minn.: Bethany House, 1971).

The Navigator Bible Studies Handbook (1978).

Tozer, A. W. *The Knowledge of the Holy* (New York: Harper & Row, 1978).

Tozer, A. W. *The Pursuit of God* (Harrisburg, Penn.: Christian Publications, 1982).

FUTURE
STUDY SUGGESTIONS

THIS STUDY HAS ENABLED you to discover some truths about God and His relationship to you. As time goes by, you will think of other characteristics of our Lord—truths about His character, His attitudes, His desires and purposes, and His concern and plans for you. Whenever you are impressed with a Scripture on a topic about Him that you have not studied, record your discovery and observations here for more thorough study later.

REFERENCES	TRUTHS ABOUT EXPERIENCING GOD'S PRESENCE

References	Truths About Experiencing God's Presence

FUTURE READING PROJECT:

Read through the Book of Hosea, noting how much God loves us as His people, how He seeks to gain our love, what His attitudes toward us are, and what He wants in His relationship with us. Record on an additional sheet of paper the outstanding verses and highlights you discover.

This study, *Experiencing God's Presence,* is one of a series of studies by Warren and Ruth Myers on God and the relationship we can have with Him.

AUTHORS

WARREN AND RUTH MYERS served on the staff of The Navigators in Asia from 1970 until Warren's promotion to Glory in 2001. Prior to their marriage in 1968, each of them had served as Navigator staff members in Asia and the United States.

Warren Myers received Jesus Christ as his personal Savior shortly before the end of World War II while serving in the U.S. Army Air Corps. Following the war he attended the University of California at Berkeley. While at Berkeley he attended First Presbyterian Church, was involved in Navigator Bible study classes there, and committed himself to being available for service on the foreign mission field.

After studying religion and mechanical engineering, he graduated in 1949. That same year, he attended his first Navigator conference and was strongly impressed by the emphasis on man-to-man training and spiritual multiplication. Although previously intending to enroll in a seminary, he joined the Navigator staff in Los Angeles for three years of training and ministry. He went to Asia for The Navigators in 1952, serving in Hong Kong, India, and Vietnam before returning to a staff position in the United States in 1960.

Ruth Myers was led by her mother to receive Christ as Savior at age ten. Following some years of spiritual doubt and questioning, she committed herself at age sixteen to doing whatever God might want her to do in life—including missionary work.

After high school she attended Northwestern Bible and Missionary Training School in Minneapolis, Minnesota, where she experienced new joy and vitality in her relationship with Christ. She also met Dean Denler there, who later became her husband and a Navigator staff member.

Following graduation from Bible school she attended Macalester College in Saint Paul, where she helped in the student ministry of The Navigators. She was involved in Navigator ministries in Washington, D.C., and Minneapolis before going to Taiwan in 1952 to marry Denler. She served with him in Taiwan, the Philippines, and Hong Kong before his death in 1960. She then served at The Navigators' headquarters in Colorado Springs, Colorado, until her marriage with Warren. They served together in Asia for many years.

She and Warren, both gifted Bible teachers, wrote this study from a series of Bible studies on the person of God that had been used successfully for years, primarily in Ruth's ministry.

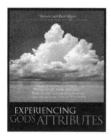